Ringing the Bell

Terri Simon

Clare Songbirds Publishing House Poetry Series
ISBN 978-1-957221-01-4
Clare Songbirds Publishing House
Ringing the Bell© 2021 Terri Simon

All Rights Reserved. Permission to reprint individual poems must be obtained from the author who owns the copyright.

Printed in the United States of America
FIRST EDITION

140 Cottage Street
Auburn, New York 13021
www.claresongbirdspub.com

Contents

Getting Autographed	7
The Call	8
The Second Call	9
Surgery	10
Cartography	11
Support System I	12
Support System II	13
Waiting	14
My Relationship to Pink	15
Cancer Club	16
Ringing the Bell	17

Acknowledgements

Grateful acknowledgement is made to the editors of the following publications in which these poems first appeared.

"Getting Autographed" appeared in Third Wednesday, issue XII /1.

"Waiting" appeared in Poetry Quarterly.

These poems are dedicated to everyone who has fought cancer in their own lives, to those loved ones who have supported them, and to the doctors, nurses, and techs who help fight the good fight.

I would like to thank my cohorts in the Maryland Writers' Association Howard County Chapter Poetry Critique Group, who did a marvelous job helping me sand off the rough bits.

Thank you to my husband Jason, for all the love and laughter.

And to Apollo, for words and music.

Getting Autographed

Before they take me into radiology,
the doctor autographs my breast
to show we're in sync,
then I'm led into a room of women.
The table I lay on has a hole
where gravity can do its job,
signed flesh swinging free.
A nurse holds my hand
while cold numbs the area
to be biopsied.
As the doctor does her work,
the nurses banter with each other,
with me, teasing about horoscopes.
There is a camaraderie
I did not expect.
When the biopsy is done
a small piece of me
will journey through microscopes and test tubes.
Like so many before,
I carry a small bit of metal
to mark the spot like a treasure map's X.

The Call

I'm optimistic, I feel fine, only
nervous from the waiting,
then in the middle of a workday,
my phone rings and a doctor
I've never heard of is telling me
the test came back positive.

He doesn't say my body's
been invaded by squatters,
hungry for my life force.
He tells me to call my doctor.
but it really doesn't matter,
his voice fades as he recedes
down a hospital green hallway.

My hands are slick, so I grab
the insufficient lifeline
of the phone tighter.
My body feels like it's been dropped
in a cold shower then shoved
into the oven.
My heart beats like it's drumming
Flight of the Bumblebee on my ribs.
I'm jerked from one life to another.

The Second Call

In a partly controlled freak out,
I call my doctor. She has to look up
the results because it seems
my G.P. is the last one to be told anything.
She reminds me to breathe,
I'm at the best end of a bad situation,
it's early, stage 0,
it will be alright.
Her calmness infects me,
counteracts the cold sweat
pouring down my body.
I write down the surgeon's number
with only slight tremble.
I start to think, to plan,
to take control,
to plot the eviction
of greedy intruders.

Surgery

For a few days before,
I washed with a disinfectant.
At the hospital,
I'm given wipes to cleanse me further,
everyone trying to avoid infection.
I need my husband's help
to wipe down my back
and I'm suddenly shy
in front of my love of 20 years.
He touches me gently,
cleans me with tenderness.
While we wait for the surgeon,
he entertains me
with phone games
and running commentary.

When I'm wheeled in for surgery,
I'm again in a room of women
and it's unexpectedly
familiar and comforting.

The sleep, it seems, is brief.
When I'm taken back to my room,
my husband is there,
sipping a soda and playing on his phone.
He's not normally patient
but today he is Nurturer
and I am grateful.

Cartography

I am a map to my own body.
Three tattoos, the size
of a single needle,
mark the path of my spine,
keeping the road straight.
Lines bracket my breasts,
narrowing the scope for the machines
as they hunt,
all the better to find what they seek.
An x marks the spot so,
like a javelin of light,
the radiation can find its target.

This isn't gold
to be found and hoarded away,
but a seek-and-destroy mission
to burn away any remaining invaders
who thought I was treasure
for the taking.

Support System I

"We'll get through this together,
like everything else in the last 20 years."

"What's your support system like?"
It's a question the cancer center folks ask.
I list out my husband, family, friends.
They bolster me with massages, laughter,
energy work that vibrates down to my bones.
I'm reminded daily of their love.
I know I'm lucky and I wonder
about those without, what
has happened in the past
that taught the doctors
to ask this question.

Support System II

I hear the story of a coworker's mother,
struck with breast cancer 30 years ago.
She had been lively, proud of her body
in a way I've never been.
The doctors were all men
who poked, prodded, and made decisions
without regard for her desires.
They tried to take her cancer
and instead took her self-image,
so she locked herself away for months.
In the end, the scaffolding
of her life fell away beneath her,
leaving her family behind
to stare into the abyss.

Waiting

Waiting is the worst part.
Ok, not really.
The phone call that tells you
you have cancer
sucks pretty badly.
Then the waiting sets in.

Wait to see the surgeon.
Wait for surgery.
Wait for results
and do those steps all again.
Wait to heal.
Wait for treatment
and the big unknown
of its effects.

Then wait during each session
of radiation or chemo,
for part of your body to turn
a burnished, darker shade
as you slowly cook it
or for your hair to fall out
and the nausea to pass.

Finally, wait for your status to change,
to ring the bell that says
you've moved from patient to survivor.
Wait for the medication
you still will take for years,
for the follow-ups
to become less frequent,
to stop holding your breath.

My Relationship to Pink

My relationship to pink has changed.
My tomboy-self hated the girly color,
the frou-frou and lace of it.
I wanted the silver and black
of an astronaut's suit
or the red and blue of Superman.

The '80s made it tolerable
but only when paired with punkish black.
As I've taken myself less seriously,
a raspberry sweater, a magenta shirt,
nothing I would admit as pink,
worked their way into my wardrobe.

Now, it's associated with that damn C-word.
People are gifting me ribbons
in that dreaded hue.
I hate what it stands for
but honor the people
who fight and survive it
and those who don't.
For them,
I wear the color
of a warrior.

Cancer Club

It's a society no one wants to join,
an involuntary, lifetime membership.
No organization, hierarchy,
badges for advancing through the ranks,
no campaigning for president.

I know the VIP lounge of the waiting room,
the proper way to tie a gown,
the secret password of a cancer diagnosis
that gains privileged access to
the sanctum of the radiation room.

I wondered if I'd earned my membership,
if my stage of cancer counted,
but once cancer cells appear, you're in.
Really not such a unique membership,
one in three will join the club.

Dues are collected with each doctor bill,
with every hospital visit, every long-term medication,
and nerve-wracking follow-up.
There's only one way to leave this club
and the dues don't cover funeral costs.

Ringing the Bell

Most days were not so bad.
I could focus on the
"I am strong, healthy and whole"
mantra in my head,
instead of listening to the whir
and click of the radiation
machine adjusting its trajectory.

Long days, when they checked
the measurements to be sure
machine and body were still properly aligned,
turned the discomfort
of my shoulder's tendinitis
into an endurance challenge
that left me light-headed.
I needed a fast-food breakfast
to ground me back to earth.

The best day was the last.
No more partial strip-tease
for the techs —
that kind of thing
knocks the shy out of you.
No more cold waiting room.
No more smiles for the tech
who knows the music
each patient wants to hear.

The last day was hugs,
wide grins, deep breaths
of relief, and congratulations.
It was a good hair day.
Pictures were taken.
Everyone gathers when you ring that bell —
it's a sign of survival and hope
for those who follow.

Terri Simon's poetry chapbook, *Ghosts of My Own Choosing*, was published by Flutter Press in 2017. Her work has appeared in *The Avenue, Third Wednesday, Poetry Quarterly, Ariel Chart, Bay to Ocean 2019,* and other print and online journals and anthologies. She's been a featured reader at several poetry reading series in central Maryland. She grew up in Mount Vernon, NY, studied writing at Sarah Lawrence College, and lives in Laurel, Maryland with her husband and dogs.

She can be found at http://www.terricsimon.com and on Facebook at www.facebook.com/terrisimonwriter.

www.ingramcontent.com/pod-product-compliance
Lightning Source LLC
Chambersburg PA
CBHW072040080526
44578CB00007B/546